Sacagawea

A Journey of Discovery

By Diane DeFord

HAMERAY
PUBLISHING GROUP

Published in the United States of America
by the Hameray Publishing Group, Inc.

Text © Diane DeFord
Maps © Hameray Publishing Group, Inc.
Published 2009

Publisher: Raymond Yuen
Series Editors: Adria F. Klein and Alan Trussell-Cullen
Project Editor: Kaitlyn Nichols
Designers: Lois Stanfield and Linda Lockowitz

Photo Credits: AP: page 12
Corbis: pages 11, 19, 31
Getty: front cover, back cover and pages 1, 4, 16, 24–25, 30, 33

ISBN 978-1-60559-069-1

Printed in China

1 2 3 4 5 SIP 13 12 11 10 09

Contents

Chapter 1

Sacagawea's Life and Times

Sacagawea (*Sah-cah-GAH-we-ah*) was a **Native American** woman. She was born over two hundred years ago in 1788 and lived until 1812. She lived when the United States was a new country.

Back then, America was only one thousand square miles of land. All of America's land was east of the Mississippi River. The land to the west was called the Wild West. Around this time, in 1801, Thomas Jefferson was the president of the United States.

◀ This painting shows Sacagawea guiding Lewis and Clark.

There were no maps of the Wild West. People thought strange animals lived there. There were stories of volcanoes, mountains of salt, strange plants, and wild creatures. But President Jefferson knew the land was rich. If America explored these lands, the country could be rich, too.

So Jefferson bought some land from the French on July 4, 1803. He called it the Louisiana Purchase. He asked two army captains, Meriwether Lewis and William Clark, to explore the new land. He hoped they could find a water route to the Pacific Ocean.

Lewis and Clark started their **expedition** in St. Louis, Missouri, in the summer of 1803. They had to cross the Great Plains. Then they had to get over the mountains to find a way to the ocean. Their expedition took two and a half years. They went by boat, on horseback, and on foot.

It was a dangerous journey. Lewis and Clark knew they would need help as they explored the new land. They would need an **interpreter**, someone who could help them talk with the Indian tribes they met on the way. They would also need a **guide** to help them find the best way across this land.

In November 1804 they met Sacagawea. They thought she would be a good interpreter and guide. They asked her to join the expedition. She was with them until the journey ended in 1806.

The Corps of Discovery

The Corps of Discovery was the name of the group of people who were sent to explore the land west of the Mississippi River.

Sacagawea was only seventeen years old when she helped Lewis and Clark on this journey. It was amazing that they picked this young girl to join them on this dangerous trip. Yet in many ways, she helped make the expedition a success. This is Sacagawea's incredible story.

Chapter 2

The Attack!

Sacagawea was a **Shoshone** (*Sho-sho-nee*) Indian. Her father was an **Indian chief**. She lived in an area of the Rocky Mountains in what is now the state of Idaho.

Sacagawea worked very hard every day. She looked for fruit and roots to eat. She cooked, made clothes, and picked up wood for fires. She helped to make teepees, too.

One day, her family went on a buffalo hunt. She was twelve years old. She helped pack the horses with food and clothes. Then they traveled a long way.

After they set up camp an awful thing happened. A war party of **Hidatsa** (*He-DAT-sah*) Indians attacked the camp. They kidnapped Sacagawea and some of the other children. They killed everyone else. Then they rode for many days and took the children to an area that is now North Dakota.

When she was thirteen years old, the Hidatsa sold Sacagawea as a slave. They sold her to Toussaint Charbonneau (*Too-SA CHAR-bo-no*). He was a **trapper**, a man who hunted and fished for a living. In 1804, when she was sixteen years old, Sacagawea became his wife.

An earth lodge like the ▶ one that Sacagawea lived in.

They lived in a round **earth lodge** by the river in a Hidatsa and **Mandan** (*MAN-dun*) Indian village.

One day some explorers came up the river in three boats. Meeting them changed her life forever.

▲ Meriwether Lewis and William Clark of the Corps of Discovery.

Chapter 3

The Explorers

It was late in October 1804. Sacagawea saw the boats arrive. Two men from the boats came to the village. They were Meriwether Lewis and William Clark, on their way west. Lewis and Clark had come up the river from St. Louis, Missouri. They wanted to build a fort to live in for the winter.

In the winter the explorers prepared for their trip west. They needed an interpreter to talk with the Indian tribes they met. They also needed a guide to show them a safe route.

The explorers met Toussaint Charbonneau and Sacagawea. Charbonneau spoke French and Hidatsa. Sacagawea spoke Hidatsa and

Shoshone. She also knew **sign language**, which she could use to talk with many Indian tribes. So Lewis and Clark asked both of them to go on the trip.

At the time, Sacagawea was expecting her first child. Her son was born on February 11, 1805. She named him Jean Baptiste. In April 1805, just two months later, Sacagawea, her son, and her husband left with the expedition. She was only seventeen years old. But she would now help to make **history**.

Chapter 4

Into the Unknown

They took two small boats called **pirogues** and six canoes on the trip. They sent reports and maps back to the president.

There were thirty-three people in all who went on the trip. Sacagawea was the only woman. Captain Clark was hoping that when the Indian tribes saw they had a woman in the party, they would see he was coming in peace. He wrote in his journal, "A woman with a party of men is a token of peace."

Soon, Sacagawea began to prove how valuable she was. She walked or rode in a boat. With her son riding on her back, she looked for roots, berries, and plants. She used

these for food and medicine. Without fresh food and medicine, the explorers could die.

On May 14, there was a bad storm. Sacagawea was in the back of the boat. She saw some supplies and important papers fall out of the boat. Thinking quickly, she leaned out into the water and saved them.

The two leaders were so thankful that they named the river the Sacagawea River in her honor.

◄ A painting showing Sacagawea using sign language to communicate with other Indians.

Chapter 5

Reunion

After five months of travel they saw the Rocky Mountains. They had survived many difficult challenges. But the hardest part of the journey was still ahead. They needed to cross the mountains. Lewis and Clark would need to trade with an Indian tribe to get horses to help cross the mountains.

Sacagawea helped guide ▶ Lewis and Clark to the base of the mountains.

Sacagawea looked up at the mountains. She saw a pass ahead. She knew where she was! This was where her people, the Shoshone Indians, lived.

When they came to a Shoshone village, Sacagawea began to shout and dance. She greeted her people. She realized her brother might be here.

Her brother was Cameahwait (*Cah-ME-ah-wate*). He was now the chief of the Shoshone. He was overjoyed to see his sister. He gave Lewis and Clark horses for the trip and another guide. The expedition left a few days later. They had horses for everyone and another guide. But the dangerous mountains were still ahead of them.

Chapter 6

Dangerous Journey Over the Mountains

The trip through the mountains brought the explorers very close to death. There was no trail. There was little food and shelter. And finding water to drink was a big problem.

It took almost six weeks for the explorers to cut a path through the mountains. At times they found animal trails to follow. But most of the time, they just had to cut a path for the horses with their axes.

The weather was harsh; deep snow fell for days on end. The steep rocks and slippery paths made every step a danger. Many horses and several of the men slipped and fell, some to their death.

Their worst enemy, though, was the lack of food and water. The journals the explorers wrote tell that they went many days without food. They melted snow to drink. Sometimes they shot a bird, a deer, or rarely a horse. But they all grew thin and weak.

Wet and freezing, they finally ran out of food. Rather than die, they even ate candles to survive. Once they started down the other side of the mountains, Sacagawea found some roots and caught some fish. She cooked the roots with the fish. This made the explorers stronger and saved their lives.

At the end of September they finally left the mountains behind them. They were headed west to find a path to the ocean.

Chapter 7

In Search of the Ocean

On November 20 they found the Columbia River. Here they met some Indians. They wore robes made from otter skins. Lewis and Clark wanted to get a fur robe as a gift for the president. It was to be a special gift to mark the end of the journey.

Sacagawea helped them trade for the otter skin robes. She gave the Indians in trade a blue beaded belt she had made.

At last, on November 24, they came to the Great Ocean, now called the Pacific Ocean. It was the halfway point of the trip. They still had to make their way back home. But they were very tired from the journey. It had been a very long and difficult trip. The members of the expedition had to decide what to do next.

▼ The route of the Lewis and Clark expedition.

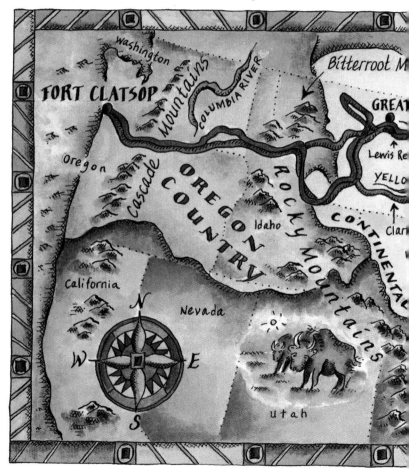

They voted to stay and build a new fort.

They would stay for the winter and rest.

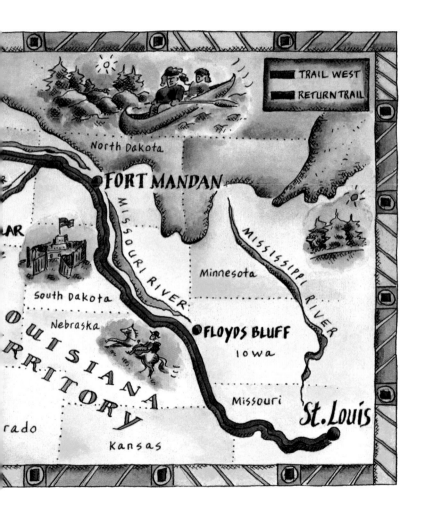

Chapter 8

Homeward Bound

In March 1806 they started the trip home.
They stayed at the base of the Rocky
Mountains to wait for the snow to melt.
In July they started to go over the mountains.
Sacagawea guided them. She said she knew
an easier way back.

They took her path through a low gap.
Just a week later, they made it to the
Yellowstone River. They learned a lot from
the first trip over the mountains. This time
they had a safer and shorter trip.

At last, on August 1, 1806, the expedition
came to an end. Lewis and Clark had traveled

from St. Louis to the Pacific Ocean and back again. They were gone two and a half years. They had traveled over five thousand miles.

Sacagawea had proved to be brave and strong. She helped the explorers speak with many different Indians. She helped guide them. And she was a peacemaker, too. As the only woman on the expedition, she helped those they met along the way know that the explorers came in peace.

Chapter 9

After the Expedition

There are very few records to trace the end of Sacagawea's life. Captain Clark was still a close family friend after the trip. Three years later, Sacagawea, her husband, and their son went to visit the captain in St. Louis. They wanted their son, whom they now called "Pomp" to go to school. Captain Clark said he would help. So they left Pomp with him.

In June 1812 Sacagawea gave birth to a daughter. She called her Lizette. But soon after having the baby, Sacagawea became sick.

◀ A painting of Sacagawea from 1810, four years after the expedition.

The records show that she died in December 1812. She was about twenty-five years old. Captain Clark had always been very close to Sacagawea's children. In August 1813 he adopted both of her children.

Chapter 10

Tributes to Sacagawea

Sacagawea has a special place in American history. There are many **tributes** to honor her. There are statues and places named after her.

◄ This statue of Sacagawea and her son is outside the state capital of Bismark, North Dakota.

31

She is a symbol of peace because she helped open the west peacefully.

In the year 2000, the United States Mint made a dollar coin with Sacagawea's picture on it. This honored her role in the history of America. There also have been many books and movies that tell her story.

Sacagawea began her life in an Indian village. At the time, most women did not stand out in history. Sacagawea was young, but she added a lot to the success of the expedition. She showed courage in the face of danger. She acted for the good of the group. Today, she lives in the hearts of many women as a role model: she was proud, independent, and strong.

▲ The dollar coin with an imprint of Sacagawea.

Timeline

1788   Sacagawea is born in an area now part of the state of Idaho

1800   Taken from her tribe by the Hidatsa Indians

1803   Sold as a slave to Toussaint Charbonneau, a trapper; President Thomas Jefferson purchases the Louisiana Territory

1804   Marries Toussaint Charbonneau

1805   Her son is born; Sacagawea joins the Lewis and Clark expedition as interpreter on April 7

1805   Successfully crosses the Rocky Mountains with the expedition on September 22

1805   Lewis and Clark expedition reaches
the Great Ocean, now called the Pacific
Ocean, on November 24

1806   Returns to Fort Mandan on August 14

1811   Leaves son, Pomp, with Captain Clark

1812   Her daughter, Lizette, is born in June;
Sacagawea dies in December

Glossary

earth lodge round home made of wood and earth with a domed roof

expedition a journey to explore unknown lands

guide person who leads others on a trip

Hidatsa the name of an Indian tribe from the upper Missouri region

history written records, artifacts, stories, and movies that keep the names of people and their deeds alive and passed down through time

Indian chief leader of an Indian tribe

interpreter person who translates from one language to another

Mandan the name of an Indian tribe from the upper Missouri region; they worked side by side with their neighbors, the Hidatsa Indians

Native American the term used today to refer to American Indians

pirogues small, light boats that had a small sail and were also pushed up river with long poles

Shoshone the name of an Indian tribe from the Rocky Mountains

sign language a language of gestures that people use to talk with each other

survived lived through a difficult journey or challenge

trapper person who catches animals and sells the furs

tributes things people say or do to show how much they appreciate and respect someone

Learn More

Books

How We Crossed the West: The Adventures of Lewis and Clark by Rosalyn Schanzer (National Geographic Children's Books, 2002)
Sacagawea Speaks: Beyond the Shining Mountains with Lewis and Clark by Joyce Badgley Hunsaker (TwoDot, 2001)
Sacagawea by Stacy DeKeyser (Franklin Watts, 2004)
The Story of Sacajawea: Guide to Lewis and Clark by Della Rowland (Dell Yearling, 1989)

Websites

www.lewisandclarktrail.com/sacajawea.htm
www.nationalgeographic.com/lewisandclark/
www.pbs.org/lewisandclark/
www.pbs.org/weta/thewest/people/s_z/sacagawea.htm

Movies

Lewis & Clark: Great Journey West (2002)
Lewis & Clark: The Journey of the Corps of Discovery (1997)
Sacagawea: Heroine of the Lewis and Clark Journey (2003)

Index